NOV 2 1 2019

Searchlight BOOKS™

New Frontiers of Space

## Cutting-Edge

# Hubble Telescope Data

Christy Peterson

Lerner Publications ◆ Minneapolis

For Erik, who helps me see beyond

Lerner Publications Company
An imprint of Lerner Publishing Group, Inc.
241 First Avenue North
Minneapolis, MN 55401 USA

For reading levels and more information, look up this title
at www.lernerbooks.com.

Main body text set in Adrianna Regular
Typeface provided by Chank.

**Library of Congress Cataloging-in-Publication Data**

Names: Peterson, Christy, author.
Title: Cutting-edge Hubble Telescope data / Christy Peterson.
Description: Minneapolis, MN : Lerner Publications Minneapolis, [2020] | Series:
    Searchlight books. New frontiers of space | Audience: Ages 8–11.  Audience: Grades 4
    to 6. | Includes bibliographical references and index.
Identifiers: LCCN 2019001061 (print) | LCCN 2019006090
    (ebook) | ISBN 9781541556713 (eb pdf) | ISBN 9781541555815 (lb : alk. paper) |
    ISBN 9781541574847 (pb : alk. paper)
Subjects: LCSH: Hubble Space Telescope (Spacecraft)—Juvenile literature. | Orbiting
    astronomical observatories—Juvenile literature. | Outer space—Exploration—Juvenile
    literature.
Classification: LCC QB500.268 (ebook) | LCC QB500.268 .P48275 2020 (print) |
    DDC 522/.2919

LC record available at https://lccn.loc.gov/2019001061

Manufactured in the United States of America
1-46036-43359-4/20/2019

# Contents

# Chapter 1

# OUR WINDOW TO THE UNIVERSE

On April 25, 1990, astronauts on the space shuttle deployed the Hubble Space Telescope. First, they opened the space shuttle's huge doors. Then a giant robotic arm lifted the telescope out of the spacecraft's cargo bay. Finally, the arm moved the telescope away from the shuttle and let it go. Hubble had reached its new home 340 miles (547 km) above Earth.

The Hubble Space Telescope (*right*) slowly leaves the space shuttle's cargo bay.

**Hubble's bus-size body holds a huge mirror and scientific instruments.**

Scientists worked for more than thirty years to put Hubble into space. After its launch, they could hardly wait to see its first pictures. But first, they had to check and recheck all of Hubble's parts. From Earth, they checked the cameras. They tested the gyroscopes. These help the telescope point in different directions. They made sure the telescope could send information to Earth.

# Seeing Clearly

A telescope on Earth's surface doesn't have a direct view of space. It has to look through Earth's atmosphere. This blanket of air around the planet bends light traveling through it. The atmosphere also keeps some light from reaching us. So we cannot see stars and other objects clearly. In space, the light that reaches Hubble isn't blocked or changed by the atmosphere. This gives it a much clearer view than telescopes on Earth have.

Earth's atmosphere helps keep the planet warm enough to have liquid water.

# Fixing Hubble's Vision

When scientists saw the first images, they were shocked. The images weren't clear at all. They were blurry. Scientists tried to figure out what was wrong with their new telescope. An investigation showed that Hubble's giant, 7.8-foot-wide (2.4 m) mirror had a problem. It was a little too flat. The mirror gathers light from objects in space. It reflects that light into the telescope's instruments. Because of the mistake, the mirror couldn't focus light correctly. Hubble seemed doomed.

Hubble's mirror had a serious flaw.

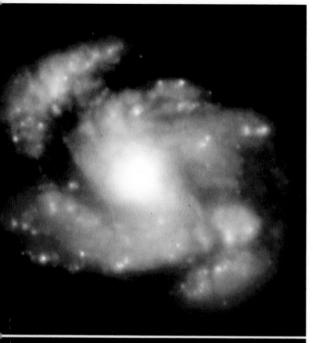

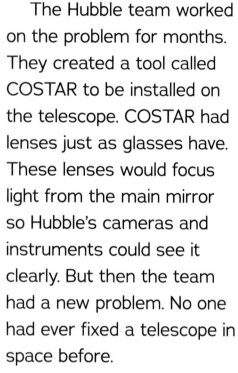

The Hubble team worked on the problem for months. They created a tool called COSTAR to be installed on the telescope. COSTAR had lenses just as glasses have. These lenses would focus light from the main mirror so Hubble's cameras and instruments could see it clearly. But then the team had a new problem. No one had ever fixed a telescope in space before.

**Hubble's image of the galaxy M100 before (*top*) and after (*bottom*) COSTAR.**

**Astronauts fix Hubble during a 1993 mission.**

Astronauts practiced on Earth for months. They used a life-size model of Hubble. They trained underwater where they could float. This is similar to being weightless in space.

In December 1993, the space shuttle's robotic arm captured Hubble far above Earth. Astronauts made five space walks to the telescope. They spent close to thirty-six hours installing COSTAR. Back on Earth, scientists began receiving new images from Hubble. The images were clear and focused. The repair worked!

# Chapter 2

# HUBBLE SEES THE LIGHT

Hubble can see light from distant stars. This light travels through space in waves, like ripples on water. The distance between the top of one ripple and the top of the next is a wavelength.

Starlight comes in different wavelengths. The wavelengths humans can see are visible light. Other wavelengths are invisible to us. The tools inside Hubble can see three kinds of light—visible light, ultraviolet (UV) light, and infrared light.

**A Hubble image shows a cluster of distant galaxies.**

**This Hubble image of a galaxy has a huge black hole at its center.**

Distant galaxies are so far away we can't see them, even with a telescope. But these galaxies give off heat energy, or infrared light. Scientists use Hubble's infrared camera to find these galaxies. The scientists measure the exact wavelength of the light energy. Then they use that data to figure out how far away the galaxy is. Hubble observed a galaxy that is 13.4 billion light-years away. That is the farthest galaxy humans have found in the universe.

## Secrets of the Stars

Hubble's ability to see infrared light also helps us learn more about stars. Stars are born inside a nebula, a huge cloud of dust and gas. The cloud makes visible light hard to see. But infrared light can escape. Hubble can detect this light and peek inside the clouds. Scientists have learned that new stars give off huge bursts of light and energy. They also saw how new stars change over time.

**Hubble took this image of a nebula with its infrared camera.**

Hubble has helped us learn what happens when stars use up all their energy. Many explode into nebulae. When scientists look at nebulae through telescopes on Earth, most look like giant balls. Hubble's images showed that nebulae come in all shapes and sizes. This helps scientists learn how stars are the same and different.

# Space Fact or Fiction

**Hubble sees the universe in color. That's fiction!**
The images that Hubble sends to Earth are black
and white. Scientists add color to the photos
later. For visible light, they add colors to match
what we would see with our eyes. But they also
add color to the light we cannot see. Adding color
to hidden light lets scientists study parts of the
universe that are usually invisible to us.

With color added, you can see much
more detail in this star cluster.

## When Light Disappears

Hubble's tools are designed to see light. But black holes have no light at all. A black hole is an area of space with extreme gravity. It can form when a star dies. The strong gravity inside a black hole pulls in light. This makes it invisible. We can't see a black hole, but Hubble's tools can find clues about where black holes are. Black holes often have bright, swirling matter around their edges. Jets of particles shoot away from a black hole at high speeds. When Hubble spots these clues, scientists know a black hole is there.

The jet shooting out from the light is a clue that a black hole exists there.

N6946−BH1
HST WFPC2
2007

N6946−BH1
HST WFC3/UVIS
2C

Hubble captured the
giant star N6946-BH1 in
2007. In 2015, a Hubble
image showed that the
star had disappeared.

Hubble helped prove that huge black holes exist at
the center of most galaxies. It also may have snapped
the first photo of a newly formed black hole. In a
picture taken in 2015, scientists noticed a bright star
had disappeared. Scientists searched the area with
instruments that see all kinds of light. They found nothing.
They think the star collapsed and formed a black hole.

# Chapter 3

# A NEW VIEW OF THE SOLAR SYSTEM

In 1994, pieces of a comet began to smash into Jupiter. Hubble's position far above Earth gave it a clear view of the impacts. It was the first time we saw objects in our solar system crash into one another. Scientists used Hubble's images to track dust clouds from the collisions. One thing they learned was that Jupiter's atmosphere had less water than they expected.

**Dark marks on Jupiter show where the comet hit the planet.**

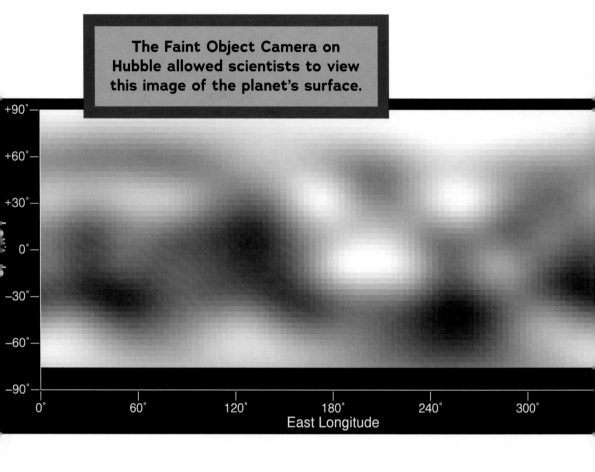

**The Faint Object Camera on Hubble allowed scientists to view this image of the planet's surface.**

+90°—
+60°—
+30°—
0°—
−30°—
−60°—
−90°—

0°    60°    120°    180°    240°    300°

East Longitude

Hubble's giant mirror also helps us learn about small objects in our solar system. Pluto is so far away that the strongest telescopes on Earth see only a bright dot. Even Hubble cannot see it clearly. But Hubble images show areas of light and dark. These gave scientists clues about what Pluto's surface might look like. Hubble also spotted four moons around Pluto.

## The Solar System in UV Light

Scientists looked at Europa, one of Jupiter's moons, with Hubble's UV instruments. These instruments detect UV light. The scientists saw something exciting. Something blocked some of the UV light coming from Jupiter as Europa orbited the planet. It seemed to be water spraying up from the moon's icy surface. The spray may be coming from an ocean under the ice. Water is needed for life on Earth. If water is on Europa, life may be there too. In the 2020s, the *Europa Clipper* spacecraft may be able to fly through the spray to look for signs of life.

Scientists believe life may exist below Europa's icy surface.

Scientists also used Hubble's UV instruments to look at rocks on Earth's moon. They found rocks that have oxygen trapped inside. Future astronauts might be able to take the oxygen out of the rocks. This oxygen could provide air and water to help astronauts live and work on the moon longer.

**This image of the moon's crater Tycho was taken with Hubble's UV instruments.**

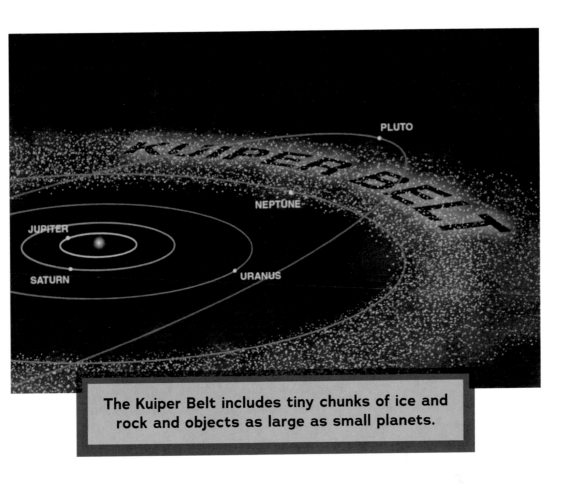

The Kuiper Belt includes tiny chunks of ice and rock and objects as large as small planets.

## The Edge of the Solar System

In 1992, scientists discovered the Kuiper Belt. This is an area of space beyond Neptune. It contains millions of icy and rocky chunks. Scientists thought they might find new planets there. Thirteen years later, they found an object they thought might be bigger than Pluto. They asked the Hubble team to use the telescope to check their data.

T WFC3/UVIS
06W

F814W

F606W

F814W

vember 6, 2009

06W

F775W

F606W

F775W

otember 18, 2010

**Hubble shows a moon orbiting a dwarf planet in the Kuiper Belt.**

Hubble's images showed the new object was just smaller than Pluto. Scientists decided that these small bodies would be part of a new group—dwarf planets. So far, there are four official dwarf planets in the Kuiper Belt. Pluto is one of them. Scientists think they will find many more dwarf planets. Hubble has shown that most of these dwarf planets have at least one moon.

# Chapter 4

# OLD TELESCOPE, NEW SCIENCE

In May 2009, the space shuttle visited Hubble for the last time. Astronauts made five space walks to install two new scientific tools and other parts. One tool was a spectrograph that measures different kinds of light. The new tool is at least ten times more powerful than the old one. Astronauts also installed a new camera that sees even deeper in space and fixed two other instruments.

Astronaut Michael Good works on Hubble during the final space shuttle mission to the telescope.

The Hubble team knew that 2009 would be the last chance for astronauts to work on the telescope. They installed six new gyroscopes. New batteries provide power, and thick insulation keeps the instruments safe. A new computer was installed too. These new parts help Hubble continue to make new discoveries.

A technician holds the Advanced Camera for Surveys, a tool added to Hubble in 2009.

In 2018, Hubble found the farthest star we have ever seen. Scientists called the star Icarus, after a Greek myth. The star is about 9 billion light-years from Earth.

Hubble also spotted tiny changes in light coming from a star. These changes may be a clue that a planet circling that star has a moon. If true, it will be the first moon scientists have detected outside our solar system.

**Hubble spotted Icarus (a small dot close to the bright star) in 2018.**

## What Will Happen to Hubble?

On October 5, 2018, one of Hubble's gyroscopes failed. Hubble needs at least three to turn in all directions. The Hubble team started up the last backup gyroscope. It didn't work either. For three weeks, they worked to fix it. Finally, they succeeded. On October 27, Hubble began sending images to Earth again.

**Hubble continues to take images of the universe.**

# Using Stars to Track Sharks

Scientists have developed tools and computer programs to help Hubble work better. One program helps Hubble recognize star patterns. Scientists use the same tool to identify and track whale sharks on Earth.

The spots on a whale shark are arranged differently on each animal. Scientists changed the program Hubble uses to map stars. They use it to recognize the pattern on each shark. This allows scientists to track these rare animals in the ocean.

A whale shark's spots are like a person's fingerprint.

Someday, Hubble's parts will wear out, and it will fall back to Earth. Scientists will guide it safely into the ocean. When its working time is over, it will have gathered well over a million pieces of data. Scientists will continue studying this information to learn more about the universe. Many of Hubble's discoveries are still hidden inside its data.

**NASA engineers monitor the Hubble Space Telescope.**

# 3D Printer Activity

The Hubble Space Telescope is about the same size as a school bus. It has large solar panels on each side that gather energy from the sun. The panels send power to all the telescope's parts. They've powered the telescope for more than twenty years! Follow the link below to download a Hubble Space Telescope file along with instructions for 3D printing.

 qrs.lernerbooks.com/dw6l

# Glossary

**atmosphere:** a layer of gases that surrounds an object in space

**comet:** a clump of ice and dust orbiting the sun

**galaxy:** a huge group of stars

**gyroscope:** a device that helps a spacecraft turn, stop, and keep its balance

**infrared light:** a wavelength of light that is a little longer than the light we can see

**nebula:** a cloud of dust and gas in space where stars are born and where new stars form

**spectrograph:** an instrument that splits light into different wavelengths and measures it

**UV light:** a wavelength of light that is a little shorter than the light we can see

**wavelength:** the distance between the top of one wave and the top of the next wave

# Learn More about the Hubble Space Telescope

## Books

Hamilton, John. *Hubble Space Telescope: Photographing the Universe*. Minneapolis: Abdo, 2018. Discover the photographs Hubble has taken.

Mikoley, Kate. *The Hubble Telescope Launch*. New York: Gareth Stevens, 2019. Read more about Hubble and the extraordinary impact it has had on our knowledge of the universe.

Schwartz, Heather E. *NASA Astronomer Nancy Grace Roman*. Minneapolis: Lerner Publications, 2018. NASA astronomer Nancy Grace Roman is considered the mother of the Hubble telescope. This is the story of how she came to study astronomy and ultimately became NASA's first chief of astronomy.

## Websites

The Hubble Space Telescope
https://www.esa.int/kids/en/learn/Technology/Spacecraft/The_Hubble_Space_Telescope
The European Space Agency is a partner on the Hubble project. This is their Hubble website for kids.

The Telescope: Hubble Essentials
http://hubblesite.org/the_telescope/hubble_essentials
Learn about how Hubble works and much more.

What Is the Hubble Space Telescope?
https://www.nasa.gov/audience/forstudents/k-4/stories/nasa-knows/what-is-the-hubble-space-telecope-k4.html
View NASA's Hubble images, and learn about the telescope's latest discoveries.

# Index

# Photo Acknowledgments

Image credits: NASA, pp. 4, 5, 7, 8, 9, 21, 23, 26, 28; NASA/JPL/UCSD/JSC, p. 6; NASA/ESA/M. Montes, p. 10; ESA/Hubble & NASA, p. 11; NASA/ESA/Hubble Heritage Team/A. Nota/Westerlund 2 Science Team, pp. 12, 13 (right); NASA/ESA/STScI, p. 13; NASA/ESA/E. Sabbi, p. 14 (left); NASA/ESA/Hubble Heritage Team, p. 15; NASA/ESA/C. Kochanek, p. 16; NASA/Hubble Space Telescope Comet Team, p. 17; NASA/ESA/Alan Stern/Marc Buie, p. 18; NASA/ESA/W. Sparks/USGS Astrogeology Science Center, p. 19; NASA/ESA/D. Ehrenreich, p. 20; NASA/ESA/C. Kiss/J. Stansberry, p. 22; NASA/ESA/ACS Science Team, p. 24; NASA/ESA/Hubble/AFP, p. 25; Andrea Izzotti/Shutterstock.com, p. 27; Davidson/The Washington/Getty Images, p. 29.

Cover: NASA/ESA/STScI (Lagoon Nebula); NASA (Hubble).